Ingrid Jonker

SELECTED POEMS

Ingrid Jonker

SELECTED POEMS

Translated from the Afrikaans by
JACK COPE
and
WILLIAM PLOMER

HUMAN & ROUSSEAU
Cape Town · Pretoria · Johannesburg

COPYRIGHT © 1988 BY THE INGRID JONKER TRUST
TRANSLATED FROM THE AFRIKAANS BY
JACK COPE AND WILLIAM PLOMER

This volume is a selection taken from *Ontvlugting* (Uitgewery Culemborg, Cape Town, © 1956 by the Ingrid Jonker Trust), *Rook en Oker* (Afrikaanse Pers-Boekhandel, Johannesburg, © 1963 by the Ingrid Jonker Trust), and *Kantelson* (Afrikaanse Pers-Boekhandel, Johannesburg, © 1966 by the Ingrid Jonker Trust).

Copyright © 1988 by the Ingrid Jonker Trust
First published in 1988 by Human & Rousseau (Pty) Ltd
Design Centre, 179 Loop Street, Cape Town 8001
Cover photograph by Anne Fischer, Cape Town
Typography and design by Etienne van Duyker
Typeset in 10 on 11 pt Bembo Medium Roman
Printed and bound by NBD, Drukkery Street, Goodwood, Western Cape

First edition 1988
Second edition 2001

ISBN 0 7981 4178 6

No part of this book may be reproduced or transmitted
in any form or by any means, electronic or mechanical,
or by photocopying, recording or microfilming, or stored
in any retrieval system, without the written permission
of the publisher

Foreword

In the Spring of 1933 on September 19 Ingrid Jonker was born at Douglas, a small town near Kimberley. Her father was Abraham Jonker, a young writer and politician, her mother Beatrice Cilliers, member of a distinguished Cape Town and Stellenbosch family.

The family had broken up and at the age of three Ingrid was moved with her mother and elder sister, Anna, to Durbanville, a town near Cape Town. They lived there with their grandfather, Fanie Cilliers and grandmother Annie (née Retief). On the death of Fanie the remaining family fell into considerable poverty, supported only by Ouma's old age pension and a small allowance from Abraham who had meanwhile remarried. At Somerset Strand and Gordon's Bay they lived an almost nomadic life under a burden of debt and privation.

On the deaths of both their mother and grandmother the two little girls, Anna (12) and Ingrid (10), were placed in an orphanage in Cape Town. Abraham Jonker later removed his daughters from the orphanage and took them into his own home.

At the age of 5 Ingrid had started writing new words to "Halleluja Hymns" and her first poems appeared in school magazines when she was 6. Her Ouma had become an ardent evangelist and on Sundays Ingrid would accompany her on long treks through the sand and bush around False Bay to hold prayers and Sunday School. Ouma read to the simple folk gathered there songs made up by her grandchild and the whole gathering sang them.

At 12 Ingrid became a pupil at Wynberg Girls' High, an English-medium school. As a schoolgirl she continued to write verse and fell under the influence particularly of NP van Wyk Louw and DJ Opperman. She was 16 when she submitted a collection of poems entitled *Na die Somer* (After the Summer) to a publisher. It was rejected, but the publisher's reader, Opperman himself, expressed an interest in her work and later continued to encourage and advise her.

Instead of a university as she wished, her father sent her to a business college and on leaving she supported herself as typist, proofreader, translator and other routine occupations. Six years after *Na die Somer* she published her first book of poems, *Ontvlugting* (Escape) consisting of 25 short poems. The main influence was that of Opperman and the book attracted little attention. But a few writers including Uys Krige, Jan Rabie and one or two others realised her future potential.

In 1957 she married Pieter Venter. She began to meet other writers, painters, sculptors, poets and to read modern poetry. The year ended with the birth of her daughter, Simone. The marriage did not last. She went to Johannesburg with her husband and child, but in two years she was back in Cape Town. In 1963 she at last brought out her second volume, *Rook en Oker* (Smoke and Ochre). It met with hostility or silence in many established quarters. But its remarkable poetic quality and originality could not be long ignored and the book has grown in critical estimation and popularity, especially among young readers. It was awarded the APB Literary prize of R2000 (£1000). The poet used her prize money as well as a travel grant from the Anglo American Corporation for a trip overseas with ideas for study and research. On arrival in England she was introduced to a wide circle of South African and British friends including William Plomer and Laurens van der Post. Plomer was a Queen's Gold Medallist for poetry and one of the top men in Jonathan Cape publishers.

During her stay in London the BBC recorded her readings of 14 poems translated by Jack Cope for two successive radio programmes produced by David Lytton and Azetta van der Merwe. In spite of successes such as these and the admiration and attention she received her trip proved to be more a misfortune, ending up with her ill in a Paris hospital. After barely three months away she was put on an early flight home by South African friends who came to the rescue.

While away overseas she had written to a friend at home: "I cannot do better than *Rook en Oker*." This was a serious underestimation.

In point of fact it proved that the poems she wrote in the period between her return and her death almost exactly a year later were with one or two exceptions on an altogether different and more profound level of intuition and technical mastery than her earlier work. But the difference was that the poems came with greater difficulty, slow and agonising. She had moved on to the dangerous region of the unconscious seldom ventured on in poetry and liable to annihilate the poet herself.

The process of translating Ingrid Jonker's poems started in 1960, often with the assistance and criticism of the poet herself. By the time *Rook en Oker* was published in 1963 some 20 of the poems in that collection (half the total number) had been translated. For technical reasons such as rhyme and structure, diminutives, children's play-words and the use of "Cape" dialect for which there were no English equivalents, a number of the poems were not attempted. Translation took on an added importance in these years from the compilation of the *Penguin Book of South African Verse* for which 96 translations were made by a team of eight poets and linguists from seven languages. Forty translations from Afrikaans were made including 8 poems by Ingrid Jonker with her help and approval.

Ingrid Jonker died on July 19, 1965, a year after her return from Europe. The work of collecting and editing her surviving unpublished poems continued during the year and the posthumous volume, *Kantelson*, was published in February 1966. A copy of the book was sent to William Plomer along with a sheaf of new translations since he himself did not read Afrikaans. However, he drew in the advice of Laurens van der Post and together they showed an interest in a collection of translations being made and offered to Jonathan Cape through Plomer who was then one of the chief readers of the firm. This was confirmed in December 1966 and the revised collection of some 50 translated poems was sent from Cape Town to be edited in London by Plomer and Van der Post.

When Plomer's "edited" script arrived in Cape Town it was almost totally rejected. In the five months that followed a lengthy correspondence ensued in which the poems were dealt with line by line. Hundreds of objections were made by the translators in an effort to rescue the poems from drastic handling that they felt had been taken far beyond mere editing. Plomer accepted all the objections. But this was an impossible way of handling so delicate a subject and a compromise was reached, not entirely satisfactory either to the translators in Cape Town or the self-appointed editors in London.

However, when the proofs arrived in Cape Town in the following May it was found that the book on the whole was better than had been anticipated. Rare flashes of significant improvements came through. Meanwhile an excellent opportunity of achieving an American publication of the book was lost. Macmillans were shown a collection of the original translations in 1966 and James Wade, their reader, became an enthusiast for Ingrid Jonker's poems. Through his contacts promises of interest and support came from prominent poets Adrienne Rich and Robert Lowell and from Elizabeth Cray, head of the New York Poets' Association. A year later Jonathan Cape's representative took to New York a script of Plomer's version of the translations and the publishers simply backed out.

The credit side of William Plomer's contribution came from his own poetic gifts. In flashes of insight he came through with valuable suggestions that have added to the literary quality of the book and these of course have been retained in the present revision and reworking of the whole script. Overcoming his problem of language, his touch can be detected in a finely turned line where the translator had struggled, the exact word in the right place, the ease and grace of a stanza. Taken altogether, his input is constructive and, while this edition is virtually a new book, it is still in certain features a Cope/Plomer product.

Poems from
ONTVLUGTING
(1956)
(for Abr. H. Jonker)

Escape

From this barred Valkenberg I had to fly
and think myself once more in Gordon's Bay★

I play again with tadpoles in the brooks
and carve luck symbols on trees and rocks

I am the dog that trots along the strand
and barks alone against the blowing sand

I am the starving sea-bird hung on air
who dishes up the dead nights for my fare

The god in pain who made you out of wind
to see in you the wholeness I'd not find

My body lies washed up in grass and wrack
wherever memory should call us back

★ *Valkenberg:* A neuro-clinic and mental home.
  Gordon's Bay: Idyllic fishing village where the poet spent early years.

Double game

Our double game diverted me,
the playful tricks, the repartee.

In my room one looking-glass
was clear, the other cracked across.

You think, man-god, you've fathomed me;
I shall so confuse you and so dismay

you'll run from glass to glass and pother:
if this is she, God, who is the other . . .?

At the Goodwood Agricultural Show

They picked me from the others to enthrone
me in this prison where I stand alone

while they, still free, come ambling by
and fail to understand my speechless cry

A First Prize hangs around my neck
but after dark, half mad, I long to trek

back to the flock, free from their idle praise
to the Karoo veld and the dusty haze

still proud to stand against the evening wind
one of the nameless thousands of my kind,

no longer the yoke of fame or the thirst
and the First Prize strung on my breast.

Poems from
ROOK EN OKER
(1963-4)
(for Uys Krige and Jack Cope)

On all faces

On all the faces of all people
always your eyes the two brothers
the existence of you and the unreality
of the world

All sounds reiterate your name
all edifices think it and the advertisements
the typewriters guess at it and the sirens re-echo it
every birthcry affirms it and the rejection
of the world

My days seek after the carriage of your body
my days seek for the lineaments of your name
always before me in the path of my eyes
and my only fear is an awareness
that will change your blood into water
that will change your name into a number
and deny your eyes like a memory

I repeat you

I repeat you
without beginning or end
I repeat your body
The day has a small shadow
and the night yellow crosses
the landscape is devoid of lustre
and the people a row of candles
whilst I repeat you
with my breasts
that take shape from the hollows of your hands

Pregnant woman

I lie under the crust of the night singing,
curled up in the sewer, singing,
and my bloodchild lies in the water.

I play that I'm a child:
gooseberries, gooseberries and heather
kukumakrankas* and anise
and the tadpole glides
in the slime in the stream
in my body
my foam-white reflection;
but sewer oh sewer,
my bloodchild lies in the water.

Still singing fleshrose our bloodsong
I and my yesterday,
my yesterday hangs under my heart
my red gladiolus my cradling world
and my heart that sings like a cicada,
my cicada-heart sings like a cicada;
but sewer oh sewer,
my bloodchild lies in the water.

I play that I'm happy:
look where the firefly sparkles!
the moon-disc, a wet snout that quivers –
but with the morning, the limping midwife,
grey and shivering on the sliding hills,
I push you out through the crust into daylight,
oh sorrowing owl, great owl of the daylight,
free from my womb but besmeared,
with my tears all smeared
and tainted with sadness.

Sewer oh sewer
I lie trembling, singing
how else but trembling
with my bloodchild under your water . . . ?

* *Kukumakranka:* Khoikhoi name for *Gethyllis afra,* a delicate starlike Cape lily yielding an aromatic edible fruit.

I went searching for the way of my body

I went searching for the way of my body
and could find only the strange scars in the dust
Tracks of blue wildebeest elephants and leopards
trampled across the safe secret of the white path
Oh I wanted simply to know your shadow, steenbokkie
and the near weightlessness of your fleeing shape

Autumn morning

Spear of the horizon that pierces the sea and the sky
morning kisses on my breasts like rising suns
through all waters you will come
all virgin forests along all pathways
in every dream of which I have no remembrance
your hands that give themselves away
and your body that plunges in the wounded fall

Morning radiance warms the bedroom like
golden squirrels on the lookout for hidden mysteries

I went to seek after my own heart

I went to seek after my own heart
and long after I had strayed from my way
in the days trailing by with their foliage
under skies blue with space and aloofness
I thought I should come upon my heart
where I kept the two brown butterflies
of your eyes and I saw the swallow soar upwards
and shadows of starlings

Lost city

In the rain that has passed by
far-off day and lost city
of acorns and doves full of daybreak

my hands were all squirrel-like
quick to be shy but vigilant
far-off day and lost city

through all the people you have come
with an unaffected smile
as if from a long journey

and the rain that has passed by
has warmed itself against my body
the rain of smoke and ochre

that smells of your clean-washed hands
of warm doves and the open
orange poppy of the sky

Intimate conversation

Don't fall asleep
>Don't go off to sleep, look!
>Behind the curtains day starts to dance
>with a peacock feather in his hat

If you call to me
>If you call to me from your throat
>a dewy little footpath opens
>in a bushy wood

I know
>Sure I know
>your mouth is a bird's-nest
>full of fledglings

When you laugh
>Your laughter is a split-open pomegranate
>laugh again
>so I can hear how pomegranates laugh

When you were a baby
>When you were a baby
>you certainly smelt
>like a little billygoat
>and flowers

Your body
>Your body is
>heavy with blood
>and your back
>is a singing guitar

Every man has a head
>Every man has a head
>a body
>and two legs
>they are trying to ape you

Begin summer
(for Simone)

Begin summer and the sea
a cracked-open quince
the sky like a child's
balloon
far above the water
Under the umbrellas
like stripy sugarsticks
ants of people
and the gay laugh of the bay
has golden teeth

Child with the yellow beach-bucket
and the forgotten pigtail
your mouth surely is a little bell
tiny grape-tongue for a clapper
You play the sun all day
like a ukelele

Ladybird
*(for my mother –
a remembrance)*

Gleam ochre
and a light breaks
out of the sea
In the backyard
somewhere among the washing
and a tree full of pomegranates
your laugh and the morning
sudden and small
like a ladybird
fallen on my hand

The child who was shot dead by soldiers in Nyanga

The child is not dead
the child lifts his fists against his mother
who screams Africa shouts the scent
of freedom and the veld
in the location of the cordoned heart

The child lifts his fists against his father
in the march of the generations
who are shouting Africa shout the scent
of righteousness and blood
in the streets of his warrior pride

The child is not dead
not at Langa not at Nyanga
not at Orlando not at Sharpeville
not at the police station in Philippi
where he lies with a bullet through his brain

The child is the shadow of the soldiers
on guard with rifles saracens* and batons
the child is present at all gatherings and law-giving
the child peers through house windows and into the hearts
   of mothers
the child who wanted just to play in the sun at Nyanga is
   everywhere
The child grown to a man treks all over Africa
the child grown to a giant travels through the whole world

Without a pass

---

* Saracens: Armoured police vehicles.

On the death of a virgin

I shall tell him you have not died
He with his body like a battlefield will know it
so that his hands reach always for the apples of the dawn
He will go out into a street without potholes
and know where to seek his heart amongst the newspapers
he will know where to find his heart under the mine-dumps
the lads the wine-casks and the literature of the stage
The cars will slam on their brakes and the murderers
thrust back their blades into their sheaths the lights
will throw a small plume of yellow crosses for his going over
The people will greet him with a vying of hosannas
He will walk like a man in clothes without blemishes
His laugh will be like a luxuriant bunch of grapes
hanging in the purple coolness under the vine-leaves
his smile recall far-off footpaths and white gables
a harbour without warships and a sky without airfields
He will know that you have not died
your death was a matinée for children
and your body a vowel for any word

Seen from the wound in my side

I looked down from the mountains and saw I was dead
My shaped temples the two lambs at the slaughter-poles of gold
and my hands the crops of doves broken with palms upwards
Oh that the word bleeding from my mouth
might give back my body its form
and the sun the outline to the hills of corn
Because the waters of my death seek the olive branches of the
                                                          sunshine
and my people the open protea of the daybreak
Over the machinery of gold the dignity of their shoulders
in the door of their homesteads in the mouth of their horses
green sunlight with feet that drag
But should they come across me in the coin
of every second that rings on a counter
in the eagleheart of the night of mutilated bodies
they would crucify me again and again who come to save them
In that I believe that it will still happen
in the borderlands of the heart
the white nativity of the arum lilies
Because I saw how you beloved John
laid your hand on the shoulder of the black man with the cross

I don't want any more visitors

I don't want any more visitors
not with cups of tea farm coffee and above all not with brandy
I don't want to hear of them waiting on winged letters
I don't want to hear how they lie awake in their eye-sockets
                                                                            while
the other sleeps wide as the horizon over his eyebrows
and what do I need to know about their same old ailments
the one without ovaries the other with leukaemia
the child without a music-box and the old man
who has now forgotten that he's deaf
the caprice of death in the robots of green
the people living by the sea as though in the Sahara
the betrayers of life with the face of death and of God

I want to be by myself and travel with my loneliness
like a walking-stick
and believe I'm still unique

25 December 1960
(on the death of Dylan Thomas)

Ward 130 in the passage on the right.
It's five in the morning for the milk-cart
has gone by with its horses their eyes gleaming
in the bayonets of the street-lights.
25 December 1960.
The children sleep
in Christmas stockings between satellites
hobby-horses revolvers and toffees.
Sleep before the sirens of the sun
before the bombers of the butterflies
Sleep in your Christmas stockings and candles.
On Hospital Hill stands a blazing tree.
Ward 130 in the passage on the right.
'Sure he drank a bottle of brandy
and lay for hours in an oxygen tent.
You know he was an alcoholic from
his first glass.' (Look there, the day's
bright gun-barrel takes aim over the city!)

'Ah yes but, he said once himself
he had a homesickness for his dead God.
His last words? Well no
he lay quiet with his eyes open.'
Ward 130. He has been attended to
the eyes closed hands already folded
the whole room like a shield uplifted.

And on the windowsill and against the light
the praying mantis in unending prayer.

The song of the broken reeds

The wind from the Torwana mountains
has her lap full of moss
She carries a sleeping child
she recites from the stars
with the voice of broad waters
against the white skeleton of the day

The wind from the Torwana mountains
shoreless without horizon without seasons
has the face of all people
has the bitter-aloe of the world at her breast
has the lamb of all joy over her shoulder
and the hangman of every sunrise in her eyes.

The wind from the Torwana mountains
with her lap full of moss
carries a sleeping child
carries a night of thistles
carries a death without darkness

and blows through the broken reeds

Daisies in Namaqualand

Why do we listen still
to the answers of the wild daisies
to the wind to the sun
what has become of the bubu shrikes

>   Behind the closed-up forehead
>   where perhaps another twig falls
>   of a drowned springtime
>   Behind my slaughtered word
>   Behind our divided house
>   Behind the heart closed against itself
>   Behind the wire fences, camps, locations
>   Behind the silence where unknown languages
>   fall like bells at a funeral
>   Behind our torn-up country

sits the green praying mantis of the veld
and we hear still in a daze
little blue Namaqualand daisy
something answer, and believe, and know

We

thus shall you die from me
like your futile seed
naked as water dazzles
like late
april
like hands naked

lovely as mortality
like a last word
unhappy as blood
not little
only
the little death

tomorrow our unquickened
seed glitters to-
morrow new girls like virgins
break against the blossoms
tomorrow
you and I die

L'art poétique

To hide myself away like a secret
in a sleep of lamps and vine-cuttings
To conceal myself
in the salute of a great ship
To hide away
in the violence of a simple recollection
in your drowned hands
to hide myself away in my word

Poems from
KANTELSON
(1966)
(for Simone)

The face of love

Your face is the face of all the others
before you and after you and your eyes calm as a blue
dawn breaking time on time
herdsman of the clouds
guardian of the white iridescent beauty
the language of your avowed mouth that I have explored
preserves the secret of a smile
like small white villages beyond the mountains
and your heartbeats the measure of their ecstasy

There is no question of beginning
there is no question of possession
there is no question of death
face of my beloved
the face of love

There's only one love for always

Ochre dusk and your hands
a vineyard through frost and Spring days
eyes of the rain on the lands, but
there's only one love for always

Instant of your dazzling body
word without language – treacherous ways
of your luminous hands, for
there's only one love for always

Green growth of the Inexorable
that sows and summers and slays
great glow of the ochre earth, oh
there's only one love for always

Tokoloshe

We children knew it all along
you eat devil's food
we like sugar-root and sundew
but each one as he should

has his own love. In the bush
one plays with water one with clay
till noontide like the redbreast
and the sun round out the day

Then we no longer see your smiles
your laugh of light
we see the dark side of your face
scared of things that catch and bite

Scared of mocking scared to laugh
we scatter from the bush
we children always knew they call
you Love, my tokoloshe*

---

* *Tokoloshe:* Playful but sometimes unfriendly sprite of African folklore who reveals himself to children.

Conversation on a hotel terrace

My death beats behind my eyeballs like the moon
I hear it surge behind the thunder of the rollers
I measure its pace in the slime-track of a snail
The days fall into the earth like sparrows
and every word has the look of Nothingness

On the open terrace we count the jubilation of the stars
As you laugh the rhythmic way of the workers breaks open in my
veins

I measure the action of your eyes at last
Hearing the day steal by like a secretive child
And if you ask what I always think of I shall answer
Child, a rambler rose, or a glass of water

Drawing

You whom I draw with a pencil
like a human secret
a letter a telephone number
You whom I draw with a pencil
like a child a naked little boy
underneath his desk at school
You whom I draw with a pencil
a word a name a cadence
I have travelled all over like blood
family circles lawmaking battlefields
like the forsakenness the eyes
of the world
You whom I draw with a pencil
but a few lines trembling uncertain
secret beyond the enigma of veins
secret that lies beyond love

Walk

The day, the pale hand-shaker
is there outside the window
I am not frightened of him!
But look at his ugly face!
This morning I'll walk in my little garden
I and my mongrel dog
I'll go to pick a rose for my home
I'll go and rake the earth
I am not frightened of you!
I'll not even think of you
I never did you any harm
Your sore eyes caused by me?
It is your own fault!
I am not frightened of you!
You jerk me out of my sleep
with every new morning come
to yawn outside my window
Have you no sense of decency?
You come just like the light
and flash your painful reddened eye
here right in my face
I should be ashamed!
Yes, I too was a child
with the sun my red marble
Oh who has won it from me
on what playground, where can it be . . .

Come my dog, you stay behind!

Dark river

Green river full of life
the sun looks into you
I can't speak with you because
you have too many secrets
Shall I talk with the small tadpoles?
They are too shy.
They tell one they'll grow into big frogs?
That's too uncertain.
Go weep because one vanishes
before his back-legs are out?
It's too unimportant.
River where the darkness
sees only the darkness
with you I can speak
I know you better

On the path to death

Your name walks on the path to death, Christ.
The heart of your eyes beats on the lips of children.
The image of your word rests in the sighs of lovers
even to the last margins of blessedness. Amen.

Revelation, significance, marrow and bones, language;
Announcer of dreams, mouthpiece of the All-Highest,
in your eyes I saw eternity without end
I descended to the uttermost sounding base of God.

Master, before the holy veil of the dawn
with my own death on my tongue I give you back
again to life, with my bloodstained name, mocked at,
crucified, the living verb of love, Judas Iscariot.

Dog

I lie under your hand – a cur
in the snarling silence
in the whimpering moon
trellised among the stars, she
in her pitiless
white coming and going

(I too still longed to go hunting hares
over my own karoo
over my burning expanses
from ochre to ochre, oh
white spaces of your hands!)

Tonight with my teeth bared I will
shake to the sly rhythm of the moon
listen to my sweetness and distance
the long-resounding bark
from my dog-box; white moon, white baas,
in the night

I sorrow for you

I lament your shadowy body
blue as your eyes shadowy and wide the sea
My hand of dust
cannot protect you
can hardly alter the path
on which your inconsolable footsteps
must rest in seaweed
My hand of dust
cannot defy the cliffs

But the seagulls can

The morning is you

Roses perfume all the air
defenceless the roses
Defenceless your hands, eyes
rose of your mouth
the morning is you
Defenceless rose of the morning
wound of the roses

All that breaks

All that breaks, fails or dies away
– like spilling of the seed in season –
has no other significance
but as treason

For all that is formed, made good or begun
– like life in the lap given breath –
has no other fulfilment
save in death

When you write again

When you write in your diary again
Remember
To look at the golden leaf in the summer sun
Or maybe the blue Cape orchid
Along one of our absent wanderings
On Table Mountain
I who have mingled my blood with the blood
Of the sun at evening in Lisbon
Have borne you with me like a mirror
And I have written you
On the open page
Of my desolation
Your nameless word
When you write in your diary again
Remember
To look in my eyes
For the sun that I now cover forever
With black butterflies

Watch-time in Amsterdam

I can only say I have waited for you
through western nights
at bus stops
in lanes
by canals
on airfields
and the gallows of tears

And then you came
through the forlorn cities of Europe
I recognised you
I laid the table
with wine with bread with compassion
but imperturbably you turned your back
you took off your sex
laid it down on the table
and without speaking a word
with your own smile
abandoned the world

Journey round the world

Olive journeys
trees water
you with your body of ferns
dreaming in my arms close by the Seine
with your body
of white gables
of bitter sun
in Barcelona
(back of the bullfights
the siestas of your hands)
Journeys of silence
journeys of walls
journeys of marble
couplets of short
hard
words
fade out but you
dreaming in water and ferns and sun
in my arms close by the Seine
go out
make fruitful the earth

Your name
(for Uys Krige)

Your name has a perambulator
your name has a boyish grin
and a sudden little puddle

What will the auctioneer say for your name?
Be forewarned

Because you're being sold
blindfolded to the bourgeoisie

like
an
old
horse

Homesickness for Cape Town

She shelters me in the profusion of her lap
She says my throat is not going to be cut
She says I'm not being put under house-arrest
She says I'm not dying of the galloping consumption of love
She doesn't know I am hungry
She doesn't know I am afraid
She doesn't know cockcrow and house-arrest are a pair
She is my mother
With cups of tea she paralyses Table Mountain
and her hands are as cool as spoons

Plant for me

Plant for me a young oak tree
in which I'll know the image of myself
and whose acorns squirrels will come to bury

give me a dog
whose paws I may kiss
at night while you sleep wrathful and well

don't let them chop my oak tree down
uproot or shiver or despoil it
give it a heaven of blue acres

put up for me an open house
so that my windows will reveal the day
green or gold or grey but well-devised

Allow at least my dog to love me
let me provide him with his food
while you sleep beyond the stars and mirrors

of my forehead

Mama

Mama is not a person any more
just a a
she gets dressed
she goes to the hairdresser
she walks in the street
catches her heels
she consults the psychiatrist
like an ordinary being

she whispers words
mon chéri
it goes without a sound
it's the white
whispering of a ghost
it has no colour
and it runs off
it giggles out of elevators
it peers through spectacles
slyly it wonders
it is disarmed
it is naked as an African
it wishes to believe in the man
who still tells of a God

Waterfall of moss and sun

Moss-waterfall
sloping sun
I
do
love
you
moss-waterfall
sloping sun
heart-
thief
thief
moss-waterfall
sloping sun
fall
fall
fall
quickly
quickly
qui
into the tiny pool
pebble
water-whorls
tranquil

You

my own
face

I am with those

I am with those
who abuse sex
because the individual doesn't count
with those who get drunk
against the abyss of the brain
against the illusion that life
once was right or fair or significant
against the garden parties of falsehood
against the silence striking at the temples
with those who old and poor
strive with death the atom bomb of the days
and in shacks count the last
flies on the walls
with those stupefied in institutions
shocked with electric currents
through the cataracts of the senses
with those who have been deprived of their hearts
like the light out of the robots of security
with those coloured, african who are robbed
with those that murder
because every death confirms anew
the lie of life

And forget please
about justice it doesn't exist
about brotherhood it's deceit
about love it has no right

I drift in the wind
(for Anna)

Free I have my own self-reliance
from graves and from deceptive friends
the hearth I have cherished glares now at me
My parents have broken themselves off from my death
the worms stir against my mother, my father
clenches his hand that brushes loose against the sky
free I believe my old friend has forsaken me
free I believe you have toppled the mountains in me
free my landscape reeks of bitter sun and blood

What will become of me
the cornerstones of my heart establish nothing
my landscape is hardened in me
brooding embittered but open
My nation
follow my lonely fingers
people, clothe yourselves in warmheartedness
veiled in by the sun of the future

My black Africa
follow my lonely fingers
follow my absent image
lonely as an owl
and the forsaken fingers of the world
alone like my sister
My people have rotted away from me
what will become of the rotten nation
a hand cannot pray alone

The sun will cover us
the sun in our eyes covered for ever
with black crows

This journey

This journey that wipes out the image of you
broken and bloodied angel thrown to the dogs
like my forehead this landscape lies deserted
Wound of the roses

How I longed to see you walk free unchained
how I longed to see again your open face
face riven and lifeless as the mire
Wound of the mud

In the nights of absence without eyes I cried
to see in your hand a veritable star
and see the blue sky blue and from someone hear
a single word

Bitter angel untrue with a flame in your mouth
under your armpits I will place two small swallows
and over your body trace a white cross
For the man

of whom you once made me think

Contents

Poems from ONTVLUGTING (1956)
    Escape   11
    Double game   12
    At the Goodwood Agricultural Show   13

Poems from ROOK EN OKER (1963-4)
    On all faces   17
    I repeat you   18
    Pregnant woman   19
    I went searching for the way of my body   20
    Autumn morning   21
    I went to seek after my own heart   22
    Lost city   23
    Intimate conversation   24
    Begin summer   25
    Ladybird   26
    The child who was shot dead by soldiers in Nyanga   27
    On the death of a virgin   28
    Seen from the wound in my side   29
    I don't want any more visitors   30
    25 December 1960   31
    The song of the broken reeds   32
    Daisies in Namaqualand   33
    We   34
    L'art poétique   35

Poems from KANTELSON (1966)
    The face of love   39
    There's only one love for always   40
    Tokoloshe   41
    Conversation on a hotel terrace   42
    Drawing   43
    Walk   44
    Dark river   45
    On the path to death   46
    Dog   47
    I sorrow for you   48
    The morning is you   49
    All that breaks   50
    When you write again   51
    Watch-time in Amsterdam   52

Journey round the world   53
Your name   54
Homesickness for Cape Town   55
Plant for me   56
Mama   57
Waterfall of moss and sun   58
I am with those   59
I drift in the wind   60
This journey   61